Columbus
Reaches the
Americas

DATES WITH HISTORY

October 12, 1492

Columbus
Reaches the
Americas

John Malam

A⁺

Smart Apple Media

First published by Cherrytree Press
(a member of the Evans Publishing Group)
Suite 1,3 Coomb House
7 St Johns Road, Isleworth
Middlesex TW7 6NH, United Kingdom
Copyright © 2003 Evans Brothers Limited
This edition published under license from
Evans Brothers Limited. All rights reserved.

Designed by Neil Sayer, Edited by Julia Bird
Maps by Tim Smith

To contact the author, send an email to:
johnmalam@aol.com

Published in the United States by
Smart Apple Media
1980 Lookout Drive
North Mankato, MN 56003

Library of Congress Control Number: 2003104657

ISBN 1-58340-411-2

9 8 7 6 5 4 3 2 1

Picture credits
The Ancient Art & Architecture Collection: 20, 33, 41
the art archive: front cover, 14, 15, 18, 23, 27, 28, 29, 36, 39
The Bridgeman Art Library: 13, 24, 25, 26, 30, 32, 34
Corbis: 11, 19, 21, 22, 31

Contents

Stepping Stone to a New World

The Atlantic Ocean is a vast sea, separating the continents of Europe and Africa from North and South America. Today it is a busy highway, crossed by thousands of ships every year. The people who sail in them know where they are traveling to and how long their journey will take. It has not always been like this.

Centuries ago, the Atlantic was a sea that sailors in Europe feared to cross. Its waves broke against the coasts of Spain, Portugal, France, and Britain, but none knew what lands, if any, lay on the far side of the forbidding ocean. The thought of sailing west into the great sea, out of sight of land, filled sailors

A European sailing ship of the 1400s.

with terror. It meant sailing into the unknown, fearful of what they might find, and faced with the possibility of never returning to their homelands.

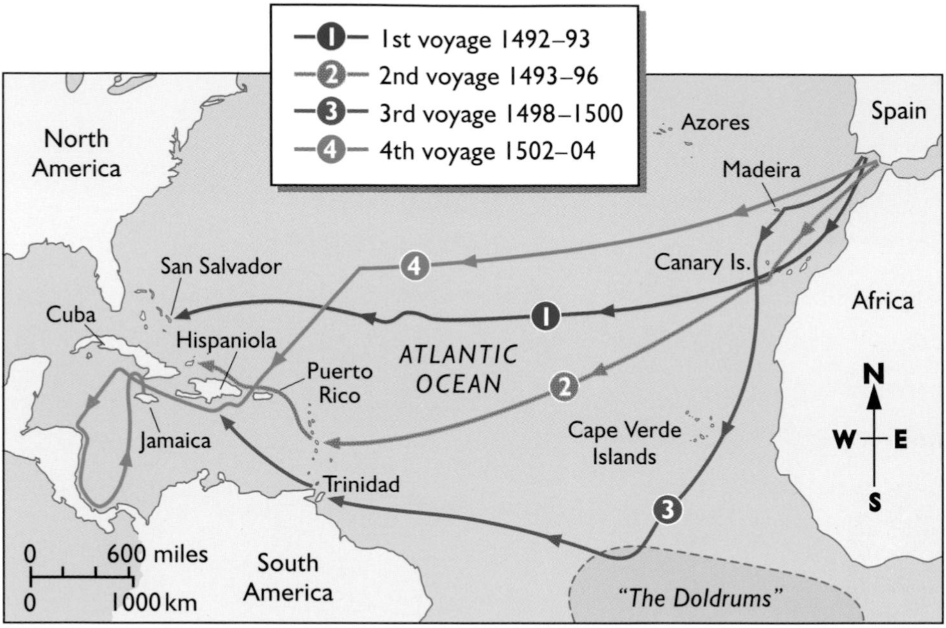
1st voyage 1492–93
2nd voyage 1493–96
3rd voyage 1498–1500
4th voyage 1502–04
North America
Azores
Spain
Madeira
Canary Is.
San Salvador
Africa
Cuba
Hispaniola
ATLANTIC OCEAN
Puerto Rico
Jamaica
Cape Verde Islands
Trinidad
N
W
E
S
0
600 miles
0
1000 km
South America
"The Doldrums"

The four Atlantic voyages made by Christopher Columbus.

During the 1400s, a bold idea started to spread in Europe. People began to believe that the Atlantic Ocean could be crossed. They imagined that the continent of Asia lay on the other side of the great sea, which would be quicker to reach by going west over the sea instead of east over land. Asia provided goods, such as **spice** and silk, that were highly valued in Europe. The country that found a "shortcut" to Asia could look forward to becoming very wealthy indeed.

One man who was attracted by the idea of reaching Asia by sailing across the Atlantic was Christopher Columbus. Through a combination of determination, skill, and bravery, Columbus sailed into the pages of history when, on October 12, 1492, after 37 days at sea, he stepped ashore on a tiny island. It was an island that no one from Europe had ever seen before. In crossing the vast Atlantic Ocean, Columbus firmly believed he had found a sea route to Asia—or "the **Indies**" as Europeans then called it. In fact, he had landed somewhere completely different, and the island he named San Salvador was actually a stepping stone not to Asia, but to a completely new world—the continents of North and South America.

Christopher Columbus, the Italian seafarer who crossed the Atlantic to the Americas.

Columbus Goes to Sea

Columbus was born in 1451, in the city of Genoa, northwest Italy. The boy's parents, Domenico and Suzanna, named him Cristoforo. In Spanish he is known as Cristóbal Colón, and in English he is Christopher Columbus.

Columbus's father worked as a weaver and a wool merchant. In keeping with tradition, as the eldest son (there were four younger children in the family), Christopher learned his father's trade. After a basic education, he began his working life, following in his father's footsteps.

Columbus grew up in a coastal region of Italy, and his hometown of Genoa was a busy and prosperous seaport. The city's ruling merchant families traded in many goods, most of which were brought to Genoa by sea from ports all over Europe and North Africa.

Wool merchants in Italy in about 1400.

The city and port of Genoa in Columbus's time.

Their ships sailed throughout the Mediterranean, trading for goods to sell, and were a familiar sight to the people of Genoa.

Perhaps Columbus's father wanted to take advantage of his city's close links with the sea. Perhaps he wanted his business to prosper by trading in goods from overseas. Perhaps he encouraged his son to take an interest in the sea and all that it had to offer. Whatever the reason, in 1465, 14-year-old Christopher Columbus went to sea for the first time.

Travelers Before Columbus

Although it is often said that Christopher Columbus discovered America, this is far from true. The land that Columbus reached in 1492 had been discovered long before he ever arrived there.

The first people to set foot on the continent of North America did so around 15,000 years ago. Groups of **hunter-gatherers** walked there from Asia over a land bridge that once joined the two continents together, in the area where the Bering Strait is today. They liked the new land they found, and settled there. By about 13,000 years ago, these **prehistoric** travelers had progressed down through North America, reaching the continent of South America. From these early settlers emerged the native cultures of the two American continents.

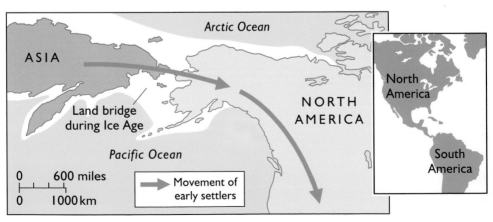

The original route to North America, across a land bridge that once joined the continent to Asia.

A Viking boat of the type that reached North America.

As for reaching America by the Atlantic route, that had already been accomplished by Leif Ericsson, a Viking who landed there around the year 1000. About 15 years before Ericsson's landfall, another Viking, Bjarni Herjulfsson, had sighted the continent, but not landed. It seems that these Vikings reached America by accident, when their boats were blown off course while sailing to Greenland.

The key difference between these early travelers and Columbus is that Columbus had a clear plan in mind when he set out on his famous voyage. He wanted to prove to fellow Europeans that the Atlantic could be crossed, and that there was land on the other side. His "discovery" of America paved the way for the colonization of the Americas by people from Europe.

The Spice Trade

Spice was one of the goods most sought after by Europe's merchants. Today, it's hard for us to imagine how important the European spice trade once was. Spices are readily available, and cheap to buy. It was very different in the **Middle Ages**, when spice was first introduced to Europe. Europe had nothing to match the distinctive flavors of cinnamon, cassia, cardamom, ginger, turmeric, nutmeg, cloves, and most of all, pepper. These and other spices were grown far away in Asia, in places such as China, India, and the Moluccas of Indonesia, which were known as the "**Spice Islands**."

For many centuries, Arab merchants had transported Asia's spices overland to markets in the Middle East and North Africa. In the 1100s, soldiers and pilgrims from Europe visited the region they called the Holy Land

The pepper plant, from which black pepper is obtained.

Arab merchants transported spice overland by camel.

(Palestine), where they tasted spiced food for the first time. Impressed by the new flavors, they returned to Europe with small quantities of spice.

Merchants in the Italian cities of Genoa and Venice were quick to exploit Europe's newfound taste for spice. They shipped timber, oranges, lemons, and wool to the markets of Alexandria in Egypt, and Aleppo in Syria, and returned with cargoes of spice and other exotic goods.

By the time of Columbus, the spice trade was big business, as was the search for a sea route to the mysterious lands of spice.

Shipwrecked in the Atlantic

The first sea voyages made by Christopher Columbus were all in the Mediterranean and Aegean seas. These were familiar waters to the merchants of Europe, and no doubt Columbus grew in confidence each time he sailed in them. Perhaps it was at this time that he gained his ability as a **navigator**, since reading charts and plotting a course for a ship to sail are essential skills for sailors to master.

An early navigational aid called an astrolabe.

On one trip, made when he was about 23, Columbus sailed to Chios. This island, in the eastern Aegean Sea, close to the mainland of Turkey, belonged to Genoa. It was famous as a source of mastic, a sweet-smelling gum or resin from the bark of the **mastic** tree. Mastic was used in church services and as a medicine by doctors— Columbus reported how it was used as a cure for **cholera**. Columbus stayed on Chios for a year, though what he was doing there is unclear. It is possible he was developing his own trading business.

In August 1476, Columbus took part in a trading expedition with other merchants from Genoa. They intended to sail to Great Britain with a fleet of five merchant ships, but they never got there. The fleet passed through the Strait of Gibraltar, leaving the Mediterranean behind and entering the Atlantic Ocean.

As the ships rounded the southern coast of Portugal, they were attacked by French pirates. Columbus's ship was wrecked, and he only survived because he clung to some wreckage and swam ashore. This was his first experience of the Atlantic.

A view of the Strait of Gibraltar.

Old Maps and Sailors' Tales

Columbus was 25 when the shipwreck washed him ashore in southern Portugal. From here he made his way to Lisbon, the country's capital. Lisbon was a thriving city, and many people from Genoa lived there, including Columbus's younger brother, Bartholomew, who worked as a bookseller and map dealer. Columbus helped him in the trade, and the brothers soon became well known for making and selling maps.

In 1477, Columbus joined a fleet of merchant ships sailing from Lisbon to the North Atlantic, where he may have visited Iceland. It is possible that in Iceland he heard tales about a land that lay to the west across the Atlantic,

The island of Madeira.

visited by Vikings some 500 years earlier—the land that eventually came to be known as America. It is not certain that Columbus heard these traditional **Norse** stories, but if he did, it is very likely that he remembered them.

Columbus returned to Portugal, and in 1478 or 1479 he married a Portuguese noblewoman, Felipa Perestrello e Moniz. They went to live on Madeira, an Atlantic island off the coast of Africa, where Felipa's brother was the **governor**. Her father had sailed with Henry the Navigator (1394–1460), a Portuguese explorer who had ventured into the Atlantic as far as the Azores islands (see map, p. 12). By studying his father-in-law's charts and journals, Columbus learned about the Atlantic and its currents. During the 1480s, on various trips down the Atlantic coast of Africa, he was able to gather yet more information—information that was to prove invaluable on the voyage he was planning.

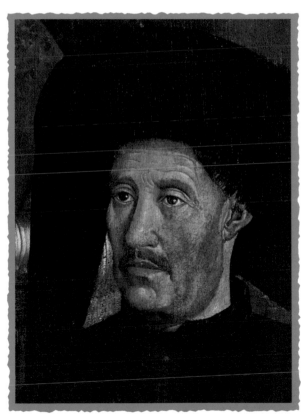

Henry the Navigator, an early Portuguese explorer.

Enterprise of the Indies

Columbus, like other sailors of his day, wanted to find a direct sea route to Japan, China, and Indonesia, where spices, silks, gems, and gold came from. Europeans called this whole region "the Indies." A direct sea route would allow European merchants to buy goods straight from the people who produced them, rather than from the Arab traders who controlled the overland route, and would boost the merchants' profits.

While some people thought the Indies could be reached by sailing around Africa, Columbus believed there was

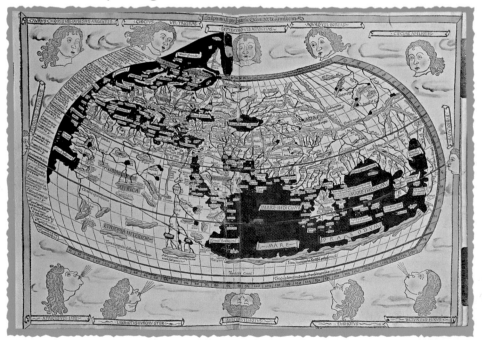

Ptolemy's map of the world, made in the 100s C.E.

another way to get there. He had studied the books and maps of Claudius Ptolemy (c. 90–c. 168 C.E.), a Greek geographer who claimed the world was a sphere, as well as Marco Polo's (1254–1324) account of his travels to China. He may also have looked at the map made by Italian geographer Paolo Toscanelli (1397–1482), which showed the Indies lying about 3,000 miles (4,800 km) west of Europe and Africa. Today, we know these calculations were wrong. The world was much bigger than anyone thought, and the Indies (Asia) is much farther to the west. As it happened, there was a landmass just where Toscanelli and Columbus expected one to be, but it was not the Indies.

When Columbus put all the information he had gathered together, he became convinced the Indies could be reached by crossing the Atlantic. A grand plan took shape in his mind, which he called the "**Enterprise** of the Indies." What he then needed was someone who would believe his "enterprise" was possible, and who would pay for it.

A globe made in 1492. It shows Europe, Africa, and Asia, but not the Americas.

25

Finding a Supporter

In 1484, Columbus took his "Enterprise of the Indies" plan to King John II of Portugal. He wanted the Portuguese to support his project, mainly because he knew that of all the seafaring nations of Europe, it was Portugal that had already done the most to find a sea route to the Indies by looking for a way around Africa. His marriage to a Portuguese noblewoman had also

King John II of Portugal.

provided him with connections to Portugal's government and royal court.

Columbus must have had high hopes that Portugal would come to his aid, but it was not to be. The king passed Columbus's plan to a committee, who rejected it on the grounds that the Indies lay much farther to the west than Columbus claimed, and that it would cost too much money to carry out.

The following year, 1485, Columbus's wife died. It must have seemed to Columbus that his ties with Portugal had come undone, and as he had no reason to remain there, he moved to Spain with his five-year-old son, Diego.

In 1486, Columbus presented his plan to King Ferdinand and Queen Isabella of Spain. Again, it was given to a committee and rejected. But Columbus refused to give up. In 1488, King John II of Portugal looked at the plan a second time and again rejected it, as did the kings of France and England. In April 1492, eight years after he first proposed the plan, Columbus's determination was finally rewarded when Ferdinand and Isabella relented and agreed to support him in his quest.

Columbus presents his plan to the king and queen of Spain.

First Voyage: 1492–93

Columbus drove a hard bargain with his Spanish supporters. Not only did he ask to be made commander of the expedition, he also wanted to be made governor of any new lands he came to. He also demanded a share of any money made from trading in goods from the new lands.

The port of Palos in southwest Spain became the headquarters of the expedition. Columbus took command of three small ships—the *Pinta*, the *Niña*, and his flagship, the *Santa Maria*. None of the ships

Columbus's three ships that crossed the Atlantic in 1492.

was more than 80 feet (24.4 m) long. On August 3, 1492, the ships sailed from Palos. On board were around 90 men and enough supplies for a 12-month voyage.

Columbus would have seen many new and unfamiliar forms of wildlife on his voyages of discovery, including frigate birds, which rarely land.

Columbus plotted a route south to the Canary Islands, off the west coast of Africa. There they took on fresh supplies, and on September 6, the ships sailed again, taking advantage of the fast-moving Canary current that raced out into the Atlantic. We can only imagine what troubled thoughts must have crossed the sailors' minds on September 9, the day all sight of land disappeared below the horizon. From then on they sailed west into the unmapped, unknown open sea.

Ten days after leaving the Canary Islands, the fleet sailed into a great mass of floating seaweed. The wind dropped, and progress became slow. It was a frustrating and difficult time, and there was talk of **mutiny** among some sailors, but Columbus convinced them not to turn back. The ships sailed on.

When Two Worlds Met

At two o'clock on the morning of October 12, 1492, Rodrigo de Triana was on duty as the **lookout** on the *Pinta*. Moonlight shone across the sea, and in the distance a shadowy shape came into view. "*Tierra! Tierra!*" ("Land! Land!") he shouted. They were the words that every man on board had been longing to hear for 37 days, ever since the fleet left the Canary Islands.

Later that day, Columbus and a group of men went ashore, carrying the banners of the king and queen of Spain. They had landed on a small island, and Columbus

Columbus and his men set foot in the "New World."

claimed it for Spain, naming it San Salvador (meaning "Holy Savior"), in honor of the Savior Jesus Christ.

He had landed on an island in the Bahamas, just a short distance from the Americas. For three months, Columbus explored this island and the other islands of the Caribbean Sea, becoming more and more convinced he was in the Indies (he thought Cuba was the mainland of China). Then, on Christmas Eve, the *Santa Maria* was wrecked off an island Columbus had named Hispaniola (present-day Haiti and the Dominican Republic).

Using the timbers of the wrecked ship, 40 of Columbus's men constructed the settlement of Navidad (Christmas) on Hispaniola and moved in—the first European **colonists** to settle in the Americas since the days of the Vikings. Promising he would return for them, Columbus began the homeward journey to Spain with the *Pinta* and the *Niña* on January 4, 1493.

This monument to Christopher Columbus is on San Salvador island.

Second Voyage: 1493–96

Columbus reached Spain in March 1493. He told King Ferdinand and Queen Isabella that he had found the Indies, and gave them gifts of gold, colorful parrots, and even **Indians** who had sailed back to Europe with him.

These exotic souvenirs of his travels created great excitement in Spain, and a second voyage was soon organized. On September 25, 1493, Columbus set sail from Cadiz, in Spain, with 17 ships and around 1,200 soldiers and ordinary people, many of whom intended to become colonists in the Indies. They took farm animals, seeds, and tools with them. The plan was to return to Navidad, on Hispaniola, and build a larger, more permanent settlement there.

Columbus presents gifts to the king and queen of Spain.

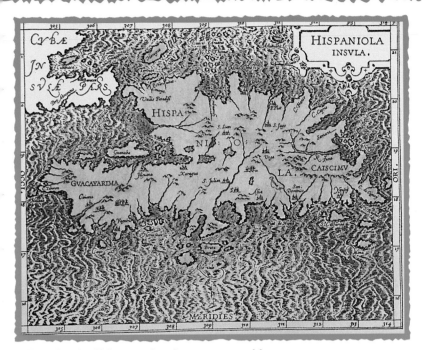

The island of Hispaniola, shown on an old map.

However, when they reached Navidad they found that
the settlement had been destroyed by the island's **native
people**, in retaliation for the settlers' cruelty. In its place
a new settlement, Isabella, was built. Before long, the
Spanish colonists turned their attention to finding gold.
There was little to be found, and discontent soon spread.
Meanwhile, relations between the settlers and the natives
were proving difficult. Fighting was commonplace, and
the Spaniards forced many of the natives into slavery.
Eventually, some of the colonists wrote letters home to
Spain complaining about Columbus and conditions on the
island. An official was sent to investigate, and Columbus
had no choice but to return to Spain to defend his name
and reputation.

Third Voyage: 1498–1500

Despite the complaints made about Columbus, Ferdinand and Isabella were more interested in hearing about lands he had claimed, aware of the riches these new colonies could bring to Spain. They granted him command of a third expedition, but it was two years before the new fleet was ready.

Columbus begins his third voyage.

Columbus began his third voyage to the Indies on May 30, 1498, sailing from Seville, Spain, with six ships. Three went straight to Hispaniola, but the other three sailed farther south than Columbus had been before. He hoped he would finally discover the mainland of China. Instead, he sailed into an area near the **equator** where the sea was still and there was no wind. Years later, this spot in the Atlantic was nicknamed the "**doldrums**."

The island of Trinidad, reached by Columbus in 1498.

After a week, the wind picked up and the ships were able to sail across the Atlantic to an island with three mountains. Columbus named it Trinidad. Close by was a great landmass. Columbus believed he had at last reached a continent, and in a letter to Ferdinand and Isabella he wrote: "I believe this is a very large continent which until now has remained unknown." He claimed the new land for Spain. Although he didn't know it, Columbus had reached northeast South America, present-day Venezuela.

Columbus sailed on to Hispaniola, where he found the colonists fighting each other. He was accused of losing control of Spain's colony, and a new governor was sent to take charge. In October 1500 he had Columbus arrested, put in chains, and sent back to Spain.

Fourth Voyage: 1502–04

When he arrived in Spain, Columbus was released from his chains. He still had the support of Ferdinand and Isabella, but while he had been away, a Portuguese explorer, Vasco da Gama, had succeeded in sailing around Africa to India. It was a turning point in world exploration. Many now believed that Columbus had not reached the Indies. Instead, he had reached somewhere else, a "new world" unknown to anyone in Europe.

Columbus did not agree, and was more determined than ever to prove to his critics that he had found the Indies by crossing the Atlantic. He was put in charge of a fourth expedition, and ordered by Ferdinand and Isabella to search for gold, precious gems, spices, and other valuables. On May 11, 1502, he sailed from

Vasco da Gama (1460–1524), the first European to sail to Asia.

Cadiz with four ships and 150 men. After just 20 days at sea, the fleet reached the Caribbean Sea, and for the next few months, Columbus searched for a passage that would lead him to the Indies. He never found one. Worse still, he was forced to **beach** his ships on Jamaica, where, for a whole year, he waited to be rescued. He returned to Spain in November 1504.

After four epic voyages, Columbus was in poor health, and his traveling days were over. In the final years of his life, he asked the Spanish government to return his title of governor of Hispaniola, but they refused. He was, however, paid a share of the money made from the goods brought back from his travels. Columbus died in the Spanish city of Valladolid on May 20, 1506, a rich but bitter man, still convinced he had reached the Indies.

Seville Cathedral, Spain, where Columbus is said to be buried.

Legacy of Columbus

Historically, Christopher Columbus is seen as a bridge that brought two very different worlds together, worlds that were not destined to live in peace and friendship. The seafaring nations of Europe wanted to explore the lands that Columbus had reached, and in the years after his death, colonists arrived in them in great numbers. Most went hoping to find gold and other valuables, caring little for native peoples or their cultures. Many natives were forced into slavery, and many more died from diseases introduced from Europe.

It wasn't only gold that was sent back to Europe. Foods that were unknown there, such as potatoes, tomatoes, maize, and pineapples, eventually found a ready market. Turkeys were introduced, as was tobacco, which Europeans began to smoke in pipes, copying the habit of the native peoples. Other explorers followed Columbus. In 1502,

Tobacco smoking came to Europe from the Americas.

North and South America, from a map of 1650.

Amerigo Vespucci (1451–1512), an Italian explorer who sailed for Spain and Portugal, sailed the entire length of the continent reached by Columbus on his third voyage. Vespucci wrote that it was a "New World," finally quashing the idea that it was part of China. He was the first to use this phrase.

In 1507, just five years after the death of Columbus, a German mapmaker, Martin Waldseemuller, made a map of the world. It showed the outline of Vespucci's "New World," labeled "America," in honor of Amerigo Vespucci. The name stuck. By a cruel twist of fate, Columbus, the man who had pioneered the sea route to the Americas, was not destined to have them named after him.

Timeline

1451   Christopher Columbus is born in Genoa, Italy.

1465   Goes to sea for the first time; sails in the Mediterranean.

1476   Shipwrecked in a battle off Portugal and swims ashore; joins his brother Bartholomew, a mapmaker, in Lisbon, Portugal.

1477–82 Makes trading voyages to Iceland, and Guinea, West Africa.

1478/79 Marries Felipa Perestrello e Moniz, a Portuguese noblewoman.

1484   King John II of Portugal rejects his request for support for an Atlantic crossing.

1485   His wife dies; he moves to Spain.

1492   *April:* Ferdinand and Isabella of Spain grant him support for an Atlantic voyage.

1492   *August 3:* Sets out on first voyage, from Palos, Spain, with three ships.

1492   *October 12:* Reaches the Americas—San Salvador island, Bahamas.

1492   *October–December* Reaches Cuba and Hispaniola; founds colony of Navidad, on Hispaniola (present-day Haiti and Dominican Republic).

1493   *March 15:* Arrives back in Spain.

1493   *September:* Sets out on second voyage, from Cadiz, Spain, with 17 ships.

1493	*November–May:* Reaches Jamaica; founds colony of Isabella, on Hispaniola.
1496	*June 11:* Arrives back in Spain.
1498	*May 30:* Sets out on third voyage, from Seville, Spain, with six ships.
1498	*July:* Lands on mainland of South America, at Venezuela.
1500	*October:* Arrested and sent back to Spain in chains.
1502	*May 11:* Sets out on fourth voyage, from Cadiz, Spain, with four ships.
1503	*June 25:* Ships beached on coast of Jamaica.
1504	*June 29:* Rescued from Jamaica.
1504	*November 7:* Arrives back in Spain.
1506	*May 20:* Dies at Valladolid, Spain.

Glossary

beach (verb) To bring something onto a beach out of the water, such as a ship.

cholera An infectious disease that causes vomiting and diarrhea and often leads to death.

colonist A person who settles in a colony, usually in a foreign land.

doldrums An area in any sea near the equator where the water is still, there is no wind, and the temperature is high.

enterprise A plan that can be put into action for a business.

equator An imaginary line that divides the Earth in two between the North and South Poles.

governor A person who is in charge of, or governs, a region such as a colony.

hunter-gatherers People who follow a nomadic existence, hunting animals and gathering plants in the wild.

Indians The old name given by Europeans to the native peoples of the western side of the world.

Indies The old name used by Europeans to describe the part of the world now called Asia.

lookout A person on a ship whose job is to watch out for land, ships, or danger at sea.

mastic A gum or resin from the bark of the mastic tree.

Middle Ages The period in Europe between the years c. 450–1450 C.E.

mutiny When sailors overthrow a ship's officers and take command of the vessel themselves.

native people The name for a race of people born in or originating from a place.

navigator A sailor whose job is to plot a course for a ship to take.

New World The name given by Europeans for North and South America. It was the opposite of the Old World, which were the known continents of Europe, Africa, and Asia.

Norse The general name for the countries of Scandinavia (especially Norway) and the language of the people who lived there.

prehistoric The name for the period of history that came before the appearance of the written word.

spice A substance, usually obtained from the dried parts of a plant, with a strong taste or smell, used for flavoring food.

Spice Islands The name given by Europeans to the Moluccas of Indonesia, a group of islands known for the spices they produced.

Vikings A seafaring people of Scandinavia, during the period c. 700–1100 C.E.

Index

12 October 1492 12 October 1492